# *HOW TO STOP OVERDRINKING*

*Dr. Marybeth Crane*

*www.fitfiftyandfabulous.com*

# Copyright

# Table of Contents

# Introduction:

Alcoholism is one of the world's oldest forms of substance abuse, and unfortunately, it is every bit as common today as it has always been. Current statistics show that some 30 percent of Americans have had a drinking problem in their past, while a further 15 percent are active alcoholics. However, some schools of thought believe that these estimates are too modest. Some people can successfully hide their habit for many years before family or friends find out. Some may even fail to recognize this problem in themselves.

Alcoholism is defined as an addiction to alcohol that causes the drinker to feel like they have no control over the amount they consume. They may spend vast amounts of time either drinking or thinking about drinking. You will learn how you can identify and help someone with and alcohol problem. You will also find information on facts about alcoholism or alcohol addiction, symptoms and effects of alcohol, treatment for alcoholism, alcohol related diseases and much more.

When you speak of good times, alcohol is almost always a part of it. In fact, memorable life occasions are normally celebrated with good cheers and laughter, preferably over swigs of alcohol. There are few people who don't love a good drink.

Across the globe, different cultures have their own favorite alcoholic beverage. In popular culture, alcohol always figures prominently, consumed and abused by the rich and famous. To the ordinary folk, consuming alcohol is a great way to let loose a little and indulge in a bit of fun.

An occasional drink is no problem, but some people need more than that. For them, a steady intake of alcohol is necessary to satiate their cravings. In more ways than one, alcohol becomes their refuge, their quick and convenient escape from all their troubles and worries.

Should this be the case for you, the ultimate solution is to switch to a different and less harmful means of escape, not to try and end escapism itself. Everybody needs to escape from time to time, even people without worries.

If I need to escape, I simply go for a run outside or go to the forest or a botanical garden. I know from neuroscience that our brains react positively to being in nature. We feel it as relaxation, and our thoughts suddenly become more precise, but behind the scenes of our brains, there is more happening that we are not aware of. My first advice to you is therefore to go out into nature and take a walk or run. It does more for you than you notice. The more ways of peaceful escape you discover for yourself, the less you need another one: alcohol.

The choice to turn to alcohol as a response to the circumstances in your life is a product of your own will. However, there are a handful of risk factors that increase someone's tendency to become alcoholic. One of these factors is genetics.

Scientists believe that a person whose parents had their own issues with alcoholism is more likely to become susceptible to alcohol than those who did not have alcoholic parents. People who had or are currently suffering from psychological issues such as depression and anxiety attacks are also at a greater risk of becoming alcoholics. Lastly, individuals who live in an environment where drinking is the norm and who are subjected continuously to pressure from their peers to pick up the bottle are also at risk of developing alcoholism.

The second one of these points, depression, can be cured — even if it is chronic. My advice of going out into nature and exercising applies here as well because it has an anti-depressant effect in your brain. You need to engage in brisk walking or running for 30 minutes, at least 3 times a week. As simple as this exercise may sound, we know today that it has the same anti-depressant effects as drugs. In fact, people who rely on anti-depressant drugs are much more likely to return to a depressive state than people that exercise.

You also need sunlight more than you realize. If there is no sunlight, like in winter, your body clock drifts by 1 hour a day and messes up your sleep. Your eyes have special light detectors for outside brightness that no indoor lighting can activate. These receptors are, simply put, connected to your body clock and the pleasure center of your brain. If it has been gloomy all day and the sun comes out even for a moment, you know your mood is immediately uplifted. Lack of sunlight causes winter depression and insomnia, because your body clock is inaccurate and drifts by about an hour each day. You brain uses sunlight to know how to correct your body clock each day. So without at least a partially sunny day, your brain doesn't correct your body clock.

The way to deal with this is to find a different source of bright light. Since normal indoor light is actually 100 to 1000 times dimmer than it is outside on a sunny day, you need to go for a particular product. Search for "10000 lux light box" on Amazon and get one. I believe a light box in the winter months, especially if you live in a colder climate, to be as essential in a household as a washing machine. All you need to do is look at the light box every morning within 1 hour of waking up. This will reset your body clock and cause anti-depressant effects in your brain.

If this is the first time you hear of light boxes and the effects of sunlight, then trust me, you cannot yet realize how powerful and important this is to your wellbeing. After just one week, insomnia and depression are gone. My old childhood friend in Rhode Island used to wake up every two hours at night for years. After I suggested she try a light box, and told her how to use it, her life changed. She was able to sleep until morning after using the light box for 6 days.

Making sure that your body clock is always on track, that you get the best possible sleep, and do not suffer from depression goes a long way of solving your drinking problems.

Note: Staying up all night is the worst thing you can do to yourself in terms of depression. It messes up your brain more than you are aware of. So don't do it. A healthy person teams up with their body. This is what you need to do. Start treating your body like it belongs to someone you love!
Of course, some people suffer fro deep depressive episodes and really need to seek medical advice, not the bottle!

In this ebook, I will show you some effective and proven remedies to stop drinking alcohol on your own which will help you overcome your dependence on alcohol quickly.

**Let's get started.**

# Chapter 1: An Overview

## Alcohol Abuse

Many people are mistaken about the fact that alcoholism and alcohol abuse are the same thing. In fact, the two are very different. Alcoholism is different than alcohol abuse because it means that the person with a drinking problem has physical signs of dependency and they continue to drink. This could be health problems related to alcoholism or social problems. Alcohol abuse differs from alcoholism because it is when drinking leads to problems, but that it does not lead to physical addiction. Many people suffer from alcohol abuse or dependency without even realizing that they have a problem.

Those who suffer from alcohol abuse suffer for a variety of reasons. Those who have a parent who suffers from alcohol abuse are much more likely to develop the same problem, or even a problem with alcoholism. Those who suffer from depression and other mental or emotional health disorders, teens being peer pressured, those who have a very stressful life, those who suffer from a lack of self-esteem, and those who are in bad relationships are also more likely to experience alcohol dependence.

## Alcoholism as a mental illness

According to the Diagnostic and Statistical Manual of Mental Disorders (DSM-III), the world's leading reference material for all known forms of mental disorders, alcoholism is considered a mental illness. Those who suffer from it often have only partial control of their rationality, particularly when it comes to alcohol intake. In fact, they are consumed by their intense desire to drink alcohol no matter what. This craving is to the point that fulfilling such a want becomes a debilitating exercise that poses a host of negative consequences to their overall well-being and their relationships with other people. Although largely a product of personal issues, alcoholism is hardly a personal problem. Their alcohol problem inevitably becomes the problem of the sufferer's family, loved ones, friends, co-workers, and everybody else he or she encounters.

However, a few misconceptions and myths about excessive alcohol intake make it difficult for some people to recognize the gravity of alcoholism as a problem. For example, some people say that drinking in irregular intervals instead of on a daily basis does not constitute an alcohol abuse problem. Some even go further by saying that since they are still able to function normally at work or are still able to fulfill their obligations at home despite their excessive alcohol intake, then technically, they should not be considered as alcoholics. Others raise their arms in resignation, saying it's next to impossible, if not entirely impossible, to change their ways and just quit drinking.

The tendency to deny the existence of a problem is only one of the tell-tale symptoms of addiction. As it were, alcoholism is not limited to the kind of alcohol you consume, the frequency by which you drink, or even your demeanor when you're out drinking. At its most basic, you have an alcohol problem when your alcohol intake begins to threaten your overall sense of physical and emotional well-being, your relationship with the people around you, and the safety and security of others.

Since you are reading these lines, I assume you have already gone beyond the stage of making excuses and may also have grasped that it is within your power to change your habits. Mental illness or not it can be changed. Realizing your problem is the opening move. Making sure you are not depressed and sleep deprived is the second move. Once both are in place, overcoming alcohol dependence or addiction is easier and sometimes harder than you might think.


Information about Alcohol Abuse

*Alcohol and health benefits*

The modern press is full of stories about how the occasional beer or glass of wine is good for us. These stories are often backed up with evidence from clinical trials.

Nowhere does it say, however, that the perceived benefits come from alcohol itself. They are attributed to substances apart from alcohol. Often, these features contain a disclaimer.

*Benefits of drinking;*

- Helps in problem forgetting-illusion.
- It is fun.
- It's a means of unwinding and relaxing, after a day that has been stressful.

*Benefits of not drinking;*

- Helps in the improvement of relationships, both with friends, workmates as well as family
- Gives room for more energy as well as time for activities and people who one cares about.

*Cost of drinking;*

- It is the root cause of problems in relationships.
- It makes one feel ashamed, anxious, and depressed.
- Drinking reduces performance in family responsibilities and job.

*Cost of not drinking;*

- Losing your drinking buddies.
- Have to find new ways of dealing with problems.
- It makes one to focus on some of the responsibilities he/she ignores.

*The biochemistry of alcohol toxicity*

The word 'alcohol' is a general term for a class of organic compounds containing oxygen, carbon and hydrogen. The members of this class have in common an attached oxygen-hydrogen unit attached to one of the carbon atoms. Only ethanol is present in alcoholic beverage; other simple alcohols are more toxic.

Unlike food, which is made up of huge, complex molecules that must be digested before being absorbed, ethanol is a tiny molecule that passes easily into the bloodstream and to the brain, especially on an empty stomach. Ethanol is toxic. Too high a dose and one of the body's main defenses against poison kicks in: vomiting. Consumed over time, however, and in moderate doses, the ethanol is diluted. This delays the vomiting reflex.

Ethanol is broken down mainly by enzymes in the liver. Consumed too quickly, the liver is overwhelmed. The ethanol bypasses the liver and circulates in the blood to the brain where it exerts its intoxicating effects.

Metabolism, or the breakdown, of ethanol relies on the presence of molecules in the cell called NAD, an important player in normal 'housekeeping' reactions in the body. If large amounts of NAD are diverted to the breakdown of ethanol, there is less of it to service these routine metabolic pathways. This can cause gout, a painful inflammatory joint disorder.

*Alcohol and the brain*

Ethanol exerts its effects by slowing down impulses from inhibitory neurons, allowing the excitatory brain cells to dominate. This explains why people become more animated when they drink. Ultimately, however, ethanol acts as an overall depressant of the central nervous system (CNS) and sedates all of the nerve cells in the brain.

In even the most moderate drinkers, ethanol shrinks brain cells. Prolonged over-consumption can lead to serious and irreversible damage to memory, vision and the ability to learn. (No wonder I have forgotten all the Calculus I learned in college!)

*Long term effects of alcohol*

Repeated over-consumption of ethanol without a sufficient period for the body to recover eventually takes a toll on the body.

Some of the effects of long term overuse include:

- Weakness and deterioration of cardiac and skeletal muscle
- Cancers of the lungs, esophagus, throat and mouth
- Diabetes
- Ulcers of the digestive tract
- Serious psychological depression
- Immune system impairment
- Osteoporosis and bone deterioration

The intent here is not to preach or frighten anybody off the occasional glass of wine or a beer after work. The facts are presented so they may speak for themselves and encourage the reader to make sensible choices.

Those who abuse alcohol ruin their famiies, work, and interpersonal relationships by drinking. They know that they are harming their relationships and social life, but they cannot stop drinking to fix them. Many people who suffer from alcohol abuse are prone to drinking and driving, engaging in risky personal behavior, financial problems, injury, and even violence. The behavior someone has while abusing alcohol is not their typical behavior, but their alcohol abuse aggravates it.

Binge drinking is considered a form of alcohol abuse. The reason it fits into the alcohol abuse category is because people who binge drink are not considered alcoholics. The people who binge drink have the ability to go long periods of time without drinking anything before having a binge. Binge drinking is what it is called when a person has more than a certain number of drinks in one sitting. For men, the number is five drinks. For women, the number is four drinks.

Some people believe that the way to prevent binge drinking and alcohol abuse is to raise the legal drinking age from 21. The age they want to raise the drinking age to is unspecified. It is also believed that binge drinking all weekend and the stress of going back to work or school on a Monday are considered to be a leading cause of heart attacks that occur on Mondays.

Alcohol abuse is thought to be a leading cause of neural defects in people who drink alcohol. These defects include memory problems and auditory problems. The people who abuse alcohol find that after a while they have trouble with these things more than people who do not abuse alcohol. Most people who suffer from alcohol abuse are considered to be younger people, though the older generation is not to be overlooked. Many elderly people do suffer from some form of alcohol dependence as well.

Addiction is not a word meant to be taken lightly. Anyone can fall into an addiction, but it takes a lot of hard work and dedication to get out of an addiction. Alcohol is a substance that some people may not think is very addictive. You can have a few drinks every now and then and your life won't change. This is true, but for many people one or two drinks can be a gateway to alcohol addiction.

Alcohol addiction can ruin lives and relationships in a short amount of time. This can be made even worse if the addict starts drinking even more out of grief over losing those relationships and making bad decisions. The web of alcohol addiction is a very tangled one that only grips tighter as time goes on.

One of the greatest dangers of alcohol addiction is not knowing when you've been drinking too much or not realizing when you have a drinking problem. Drinking is such a common part of our lives that it's easy to downplay how much you've actually consumed and not see a problem. Even low amounts of alcohol can affect your body, personality and judgment to a degree, but many drinkers don't want to make a fuss out of a few drinks.

Many people have too much pride to admit that they have problems to work through to begin with. They may try to blame outside sources like a spouse or a job instead of taking responsibility for themselves and their actions.

If you suspect you may be living with or know someone with an alcohol addiction, learn the initial warning signs in order to solidify your suspicions.

Alcohol addicts aren't just people who drink on a regular basis; they're people with a true physical dependence on alcohol. Alcohol addicts will have regular cravings for alcoholic beverages and may become irritated if these cravings can't be fed. Alcohol addicts also seem to have difficulty learning how to limit what they drink. Alcohol addicts may have a huge tolerance for alcohol, which can be extremely dangerous. Alcohol addicts who have a high tolerance for alcohol run a high risk of drinking more than they can handle. This can lead to severe intoxication and may even lead to alcohol poisoning, which can be fatal. One way to spot a gradual descent into alcohol addiction is a need to consume more alcohol than usual in order to get drunk.

A sign of severe alcohol addiction is getting symptoms of withdrawal when you go for an extended period without a drink. Cold sweats, shaking, nausea and more are all signs of withdrawal and immediate action should be taken for anyone showing these symptoms.

Alcohol addiction doesn't have to be a dead end road. Admission is seen by many as the hardest part of recovery. Once you've admitted that you have an alcohol addiction, you can get the help you need. There are many rehab centers and clinics available as well as family and friends to help you through your addiction.

## Why You Need to Stop Excessive Alcohol Drinking

### Drinking (Alcohol-Related Diseases)

If you drink alcohol on a regular basis, then you should definitely consider quitting or at lea decreasing your drinking to an occasional level. Some people can do this, others cannot. Excessive alcohol intake has been linked to several health problems. Below are some of the many health conditions that are associated with excessive alcohol use:

### Anemia

If you drink regularly, then you are probably lowering the number of red blood cells in your body. Over time, this can cause a condition called anemia. Fatigue, lightheadedness and shortness of breath are some of the most common signs of anemia. Anemia is relatively easy to treat in most cases. However, if anemia is not treated, then it can cause a heart attack.

*Heart Disease*

Heart disease kills more people in the United States each year than any other health condition. Heavy drinking can make you more susceptible to developing heart disease. In fact, a study done by a research group at Harvard University showed that heavy drinkers have twice as many heart attacks as non-drinkers. When you drink heavily, it causes the platelets in your blood to clump together and form clots. Blood clots make you more susceptible to having a stroke or heart attack.

Additionally, heavy drinking puts you at risk for developing cardiomyopathy. Cardiomyopathy is a condition that causes the heart muscle to deteriorate. Eventually, the heart muscle will weaken, and this can cause an abnormal heart rhythm. Abnormal heart rhythms often lead to sudden death.

*Cirrhosis*

The liver is the organ that is responsible for breaking down toxic substances in the body. Approximately 90 to 98 percent of the alcohol that you consume is broken down by your liver. The liver is very efficient at breaking down alcohol, but over time, excessive alcohol intake can severely damage the liver cells. As a result of this, a condition called cirrhosis develops. Cirrhosis causes the liver to scar and function poorly. Once the liver has been scarred, it cannot return to normal.

Most people with cirrhosis will eventually need a liver transplant. Unfortunately, the vast majority of these patients die while they are waiting for an available liver. It is estimated that 29,000 people in the United States die from cirrhosis.

*Dementia*

As you get older, your brain begins to shrink, and that is completely normal. However, if you drink heavily, then your brain will shrink at a much faster rate. This can put you at risk for developing dementia, which is a condition that causes memory loss and confusion. Even though this condition typically develops in older people, there have been cases reported of people who developed this condition while they were in their 30s.

*Infectious Diseases*

When you drink alcohol, you are much more likely to make poor decisions. This can put you at risk for developing HIV or another sexually-transmitted disease. In fact, studies have shown that heavy drinkers are three times more likely to develop an STD. Furthermore, excessive drinking suppresses your immune system. Not only are you more likely to develop infectious illnesses, but your body will also have a hard time fighting those illnesses.

*Nutrient Deficiency and Dehydration*

After even a short time of excessive drinking, alcoholics may start to look haggard, sallow and unhealthy. They may also exhibit reduced cognitive performance and low energy. Much of this is due to the fact that alcohol depletes many critical nutrients from the body. Zinc, vitamin C and water are essential to good skin health, so physical appearance is often the first thing that suffers when their levels become too low. Magnesium, sodium, B vitamins, calcium and potassium are important for energy production and nervous system function, so a deficiency in these can be blamed for cognitive impairment and fatigue.

Metabolizing alcohol places considerable strain on the body, causing nutrient stores to be rapidly consumed. The nutrient levels most affected are the electrolytes calcium, magnesium and sodium. Because these minerals support the nervous system, deficiency can contribute to heart attack, mental problems, neuropathy, and other forms of nervous system damage. The body's B vitamin stores are also used up. This vitamin group is essential for nervous system maintenance, mood, energy production, and healthy metabolism. Furthermore, zinc, which is critical for breaking down alcohol for excretion, is also depleted by drinking. When levels are too low, the metabolites of alcohol linger in the body, allowing them to cause more damage.

*Blood Sugar Imbalance*

One effect of alcohol that mainstream medicine often fails to consider is its impact on blood sugar levels. The fact that alcohol is poisonous means that your body's top priority is to get rid of it as quickly as possible. In order to achieve this, your body shifts resources away from other processes. In this case, it stops trying to maintain a healthy blood glucose range. Drinking also stimulates the secretion of insulin, which over time can result in insulin resistance. This dramatically increases the risk of metabolic syndrome, weight gain, diabetes and alcoholic liver disease. In fact, an estimated 45 to 70 percent of alcoholics with liver disease also suffer from either insulin resistance or diabetes.

*Further Blood Sugar Problems*

Heavy drinking severely disturbs the body's ability to regulate blood glucose. This is believed to be responsible for several alcoholism-related diseases, such as alcoholic liver disease, diabetes, metabolic syndrome, liver inflammation and fat gain. In addition, low blood sugar, a condition that often occurs during alcohol withdrawal, is also capable of causing violent mood swings, fatigue, cravings for sugar and alcohol and frequent urination

*Stress Levels and Mood Impact*

If you think that having a few drinks after a bad day will help you get over it, think again. Studies have shown that consuming alcohol after a negative experience causes it to be more deeply imprinted into your mind. This can cause you to dwell on the situation and blow it out of proportion, possibly causing you to react in an unreasonable manner. Alcohol abuse is also closely associated with most major mood disorders, such as depression, anxiety, and anger issues. To make matters worse, prolonged alcohol consumption increases levels of cortisol, the stress hormone. High cortisol leads to fat gain, difficulty losing weight, hormonal imbalance, inflammation, low energy, heart disease and various degenerative illnesses.

*Further Unstable Mood Issues*

Alcohol can have unpredictable effects on mood. It might make someone feel happy and positive one time but cause them to become hateful and belligerent the next. It also affects everyone differently. Some people will reliably become aggressive and angry each time they over-imbibe. Furthermore, alcohol's short half-life in the body means that, for chronic drinkers, withdrawal symptoms can occur mere hours after drinking. The constant cycle of consumption and withdrawal often results in dramatic mood changes.

*Night Sweats*

Although soaking the bed with sweat each night sounds more like an inconvenience than a health risk, it should be taken seriously. Nobody seems to agree on exactly what causes night sweats, but there is some evidence that fluctuations in blood sugar may be to blame. The biggest threat behind this occurrence is that it exacerbates both the advanced dehydration and nutrient deficiency often seen with alcohol abuse. Furthermore, night sweats may also cause the sufferer to awaken multiple times throughout the night, resulting in suboptimal sleep quality and poor recovery from drinking sprees.

## Symptoms of Alcoholism

Before I continue with solutions to alcoholism, I want to take a step back. After all, it may be that you are not the one suffering from it, but instead have a friend or family member in this condition. Perhaps you bought this book to get a better understanding of it all.

For this eventuality, I want to talk a bit about how you can tell if someone is suffering from alcohol addiction. Here are a few common signs:

*Denial of the problem*

One of the hallmark symptoms of any form of addiction is the tendency to deny the existence of a problem. Indeed, addicts tend to underplay the host of negative effects their addiction has on themselves and the people around them, or else conveniently pass the blame on others.

This is most certainly the case for those suffering from alcohol abuse. Despite consuming more alcohol than they can physically endure, they remain insistent that they are not drinking too much. When accused that they have an alcohol problem, they flat out reject such a notion. Instead, they instinctively switch to defensive mode by claiming that others are merely blowing things out of proportion. If they do agree to such notion, it's usually someone or something else's fault. They agree with the suggestion that it's something that happened not out of their own free will, but because they were inevitably pushed to turn to alcohol by circumstances and the people around them.

In more ways than one, this denial serves as a way for alcoholics to justify or rationalize their behavior. By choosing to believe that they are not doing anything wrong or troublesome, either to themselves or others, they get the affirmation that they need to carry on with their behavior without feeling guilty or being overly conscious. In truth, however, this sense of denial can only last so long before it eventually gets ripped by the more damaging effects of alcoholism later on.

*Spending too much time drinking*

In general, an addiction is anything taken in excess of what is considered normal and acceptable, to the point that it becomes detrimental to one's overall sense of well-being. For those with issues relating to alcohol abuse, this means engaging in binge drinking without the slightest regard for the consequences such an unhealthy behavior may bring over the short and long term. Indeed, for alcoholics, everything else is relegated below their ultimate priority, which is to satiate their taste for alcohol whenever or wherever they may be.

*Tendency to lie to cover up alcohol abuse*

It's not uncommon to hear stories of married people telling their spouses that they will be out late for overtime or a business event when in fact they will be out drinking. Of course, this is only one example of how those suffering from alcoholism will go to great lengths to cover up their predilection to consume alcohol, even if this means lying to the people they love. Don't take even the smallest lie lightly. The fact that they have to resort to making up stories just goes to show that they are completely aware that whatever they're doing is not going to sit well with the people they are trying to hide it from. This is another tell-tale sign that their alcohol consumption is going too far.

*Inability to control urges*

An almost palpable sense of helplessness is apparent among those who have a drinking problem. Similar to those suffering from other forms of addiction, alcoholics cannot willfully muster the motivation or energy to say "no" to their urges. This is because their mind is conditioned to view alcohol intake as an extremely satisfying behavior. As such, everything else just would not give them the same kind of high or satisfaction that they get when intoxicated.

*Neglect of responsibilities at home, school, or at work*

Since everything else in the life of an alcoholic is now relegated below the hierarchy of priorities wherein alcohol consumption comes out on top, there is a marked neglect of one's duties and obligations to family and friends, as well as a noticeably dismal performance at work or at school. Alcoholism, or any other form of addiction for that matter, negatively alters one's sense of focus and concentration to the point that one disengages from everything else as he or she gets buried deep in alcohol dependence. This apparently leads to social withdrawal, reduced productivity at work, and failing marks at school.

Alcohol is widely known for its ability to cause impulsive and irrational behavior. The fact that it lowers inhibitions means that it becomes very easy to ignore important responsibilities. For example, someone who is addicted to alcohol might shun friends, fail to keep appointments or even skip out on work or school in favor of getting drunk. Obviously, this sort of behavior can have serious consequences.

*Spending too much money on alcohol*

Money is a non-issue for alcoholics when it comes to satisfying their alcohol cravings. As it were, a large part of their earnings is automatically diverted toward alcohol consumption to the detriment of far more important expenditures, such as utilities and food, which get severely compromised as a result.

In low income families, people can get so heavily indebted that they find themselves selling their possessions, or worse, stealing from others just to satiate their craving. If you notice that someone who doesn't have much money spends a lot on alcohol, you can be fairly sure they have a drinking problem.

*Increasing alcohol tolerance*

The mind gets easily accustomed to habits; it develops tolerance to the usual things over time. This is precisely the reason why addiction is the kind of problem that naturally progresses from worse to worst, particularly when left unchecked. If you get a high after a round of, say, three bottles of beer, sooner or later your mind gets used to this amount of alcohol, so much so that you have to increase your intake to four or five bottles to achieve the same high. Indeed, as your mind and body develop greater tolerance to alcohol, the greater amount of alcohol you need to drink to feel high.

If you notice someone drinks a lot before effects happen, you can be sure they are drinking too much in general. Otherwise, they would not have this level of tolerance.

*Depression and Anxiety*

Another tell-tale sign of addiction is when people become subject to negative feelings, such as distress and extreme restlessness, once the addictive substance is taken out of the equation. They have gotten so used to indulging in this substance that their minds and bodies find it difficult to deal without it. This situation can turn into a condition known as withdrawal syndrome.

Fortunately, for all the negative effects alcoholism has on one's self and on others, it is a condition that is entirely treatable. In the next chapter, I give an outline of some concrete measures and strategies that can be done to kick-start the recovery process.

As mentioned in the introduction according to statistical data, an estimated 15 percent of American adults struggle with a drinking problem. Furthermore, some 30 percent of Americans also admit to having had a drinking problem at some point in their lives. Unfortunately, the actual numbers may be much higher.

Because of this, it's important to be able to recognize the symptoms of alcoholism so that treatment may begin as soon as possible.

While drinking may seem uplifting at first, the toxicity of the alcohol quickly takes hold. Prolonged drinking eventually causes levels of happiness-inducing neurotransmitters, namely serotonin and dopamine, to plummet. The result is an inability to enjoy activities, feeling hopeless, a lack of motivation, guilt, anger and frustration. Much of the time, feelings of anxiety accompany the depression and tend to be more intense the longer drinking continues.

# Chapter 3: Concrete Measures to End Overdrinking

As stated in the introduction part, the journey to stop alcoholism and alcohol abuse or dependence requires self-commitment. This is not something that you can do overnight and expect to be successful. Maybe you can decide to change and transform suddenly but be sure you won't make any big change in your life. Alcohol "quitting, recovery and treatment" is a process that requires gradual handling.

During the initial stages of alcohol stoppage you will be required to have self-denial. There will be the hangovers, craves as well as yearn to be in the company of alcohol and your alcoholic friends. Many people admit to their friends and families that they have made the decision to stop and quit drinking, but end up getting back to it quickly with some excuses. When deciding you should not drag yourself backward, in the name of partying or a bash.

Thinking about the benefits of drinking and not drinking; think about the costs of drinking and not drinking, rate the two. Which is one benefits you? Which one is expensive? Perhaps, drinking goes on the negative sides for both the two cases. You can take a pen and a paper then write the answers to the following question. That is while drinking and while not drinking; after that perform an evaluation and then decide whether to or not to quit drinking.

There are no medical cures for alcoholism, but this should not deter you from having a genuine desire to quit drinking. There are a number of approaches that you can choose from to effectively inhibit yourself from succumbing to some of the old behavioral patterns that push you to drink. We shall first look at these approaches, before I explain my favorite technique in the final chapter of this book.

Any treatment or healing process designed to overcome alcohol abuse need to begin with the admission of a problem and a sincere willingness to change for the better. In the absence of the resolve to change things, it would be very difficult to get past your addiction or dependence without the risk of eventually falling back into a relapse.

In war, business, and personal change, one needs to make a total commitment.

## How to Get Started Creating Goals

Begin by creating a set of realistic and reasonable goals to guide you as you go along. These goals will lend a direction as to where and how you want to see yourself in the days ahead. In creating your goals, acknowledge your own limitations. This is because it is so easy to create lofty goals, but these are normally very hard to follow through.

For instance, saying you want to be sober for a year may sound pretty reasonable until you realize that a full year is far too long a period of time, and that a lot of things can happen in between. Of course this is not to say it's impossible to maintain sobriety for a year — far from it. The only point here is that setting your sights on a difficult goal can be made easier by creating a set of small and attainable goals.

A better way to go about it is by starting with a weekly goal. Once you have reached this goal, you can aim for something more significant, such as staying alcohol-free for a full month. As you progress, create a quarterly goal. Being sober for half a year is the next logical sequence, and before you know it, you're on your way to being free from alcohol for a year. The series of little successes you have managed to achieve over the course of a year can all add up to give you the necessary motivation and drive to get you going.

*Don't talk about it*

See, if you tell people about your goals, they are likely to praise you, wish you good luck, or something along those lines. This experience, however, is like a positive outcome and activates the pleasure center in your brain. You automatically feel like you already achieved something and are less likely to go through with it. Studies have demonstrated that people who get praised after telling others about their goals feel they are already well on their way to success, while people that don't tell feel they still have a long way to go.

So consider not sharing your goals and daily or weekly achievements with friends or on Internet forums. Just do it and you are much more likely to succeed.

*Identifying and managing triggers*

You should also be fully aware of the factors that trigger your desire to turn to alcohol for comfort or some semblance of escape. In order to effectively map out a blueprint designed to address your alcohol problem, you should be fully cognizant of these so-called triggers, for alcoholism as a problem doesn't rise out of nowhere. It has to come from somewhere. These triggers are precisely the things that you should be on top of if you want to end your dependence on alcohol.

Some of the common triggers for alcohol abuse are stress, emotional issues, financial problems, low self-esteem, inability to handle loneliness or disappointments, and family troubles. In general, handling any of these admittedly complex issues requires strong will and an ample dose of positivity. Later in the succeeding chapters, I will give you a couple of pointers on how to integrate positivity and strong will as components of your lifestyle.

On your own, there are a lot of measures that you can do in order to kick-start your recovery from unhealthy alcohol intake.

Remove all forms of alcoholic drinks from your home. If you intend to be sober over the long term, there are no ifs and buts with regard to this. Be uncompromising as you sweep up your place for anything that might cause you to fall into a relapse. Check every nook and cranny to make sure nothing is left behind. Once done, pour down the drain all the alcohol you've managed to find. Don't feel bad about throwing away pricey liquor.

Stay away from bars, clubs, or any setting where alcohol is served. This may come across as a tall order, but you really don't have much choice. Going to the usual watering hole only makes it difficult for you to control your urges and resist the social pressure to down a few shots with other people.

Create a new routine. If you have gotten so used to your previous schedule where a particular time of the day had been allotted specifically for drinking, then shake up your routine and create a new one. This way, you get to disabuse yourself of the idea that you have to drink at a particular time of day.

Reconsider who your friends are. It might surprise you that you and the people you hang out with most of the time share only one common trait, and that is your love for alcohol. Think about it for a second and try to understand if this is what friendship means. If you are out to stop being dependent on alcohol, you're probably better off without your drinking buddies.

Whenever you feel like grabbing a bottle or two (or more), think of the immediate negative consequences you are set to encounter. For example, the money you just spent on a drink could have been part of your savings. Additionally, if your family knows about your goal, you would disappoint them. Most of the things humans do is to avoid pain and get pleasure. So by imagining and concentrating on some other pain, the pain of having to stay away from alcohol becomes more bearable.

Reinforce your desire to steer clear of any alcoholic beverage by associating it with negative imagery. Going through blackouts, doing stupid things, vomiting in public spaces, and hurting yourself and other people are just some of the lousy stuff that can happen if you decide to drink again. Remember to always take full control of your urges.

And as always, consult with a medical practitioner to find out the healthiest way to quit alcohol. If you are a really heavy drinker, going cold turkey in a snap may pose a series of adverse side effects symptomatic of withdrawal syndrome. Some experts believe that from a medical perspective, gradually decreasing the amount of alcohol consumed is a far better option than just deciding to completely ditch alcohol in one fell swoop. The dynamics of withdrawal syndrome are discussed in detail in the next chapter.

With proper evaluation of both the instances, you will find that drinking has got no good benefits. It is also evident and clear that drinking costs you a lot. It makes you not to focus on what you are supposed to, through the creation of delusion in your mind. Perhaps, losing friends that you have been drinking with can be apparently costly. However, look, you can still get good friends that are focus in other areas of life who will ultimately assist you to fulfill your new plans and goal. In case you are a teen, consider engaging in games, movies and outs including life adventures. You will never imagine how wonderful your life can turn out to be!

When a person suffers from alcohol dependence or alcoholism, it is entirely possible that they can overcome their drinking habits and begin the recovery process. In fact, studies show that approximately 50 to 60 percent of the people who make it through one year of recovery will remain free of alcohol for the rest of their lives. Others might have one or more relapses, but each time they become stronger and more able to overcome their addiction or abuse. The people who remain sober for life are the ones who have a good support system in their friends, family, and alcohol support groups. People who do not have support from their friends and family are the ones who are more likely to relapse.

No one can stop drinking until they realize and admit that they have a problem with alcohol. Unfortunately, most people with drinking problems are not aware of the fact that their drinking is a problem. Many of these people assume that they have the ability to stop drinking at any time, but that they don't want to stop at the moment. Alcohol addiction is a process, and the process has to start somewhere.

Once a person with an alcohol problem admits the problem, stops drinking, and seeks help, the recovery process can begin. The first step is detoxification and withdrawal. During this process medical professionals administer medication to the addict to help them deal with withdrawal symptoms, such as visions and hallucinations. From this point on, the recovery period consists of counseling.

During counseling, the person who suffers from alcohol dependence or alcoholism learns what makes them tick. At some point in their life, alcoholics go through something that causes them to turn to alcohol as a coping method. When the person who suffers from alcoholism or abuse learns what this is, they can learn how to avoid situations that mimic it and how to deal with it in a healthier manner. Group counseling sessions allow addicts and abusers to share their stories. They share how they got started drinking, why they drank, what they did when they drank, and what caused them to make the decision to stop drinking. People with alcoholism or abuse problems will hear the stories of other people just like them, and they can all lean on one another for support.

This form of support is just as important as the support that addicts and abusers receive from their families. These supporters are there for each other throughout the recovery process, which lasts forever.

## Stop Drinking: Fully or Gradually?

Analyzing the severity of the problems associated with your drinking can give you the best answer for this question. This will include rating the amount of time you have been drinking, how you much you spend, how much you have been drinking,  to mention just but a few cases. It is also important to note the fact that alcoholism means that you are not able to get a good control of yourself when drinking as well as the drinking itself. Thus, for any alcoholic person it is good to make a decision and stop it completely. Those without a physical dependency may just gradually decrease their alcohol intake and see if they can control it.

According to the National Institute on Alcohol Abuse and Alcoholism, making a decision of cutting drinking is recommended when you want to quit drinking due to health and personal reasons. This will give your body and mind a time to cope with the new situation and get rid of the anxiety that would be associated with drinking. Considering setting a self drinking plan or goal can make it effective. As said earlier make a choice of drinking two bottles a day, got to one bottle and then half, from there you can easily quit. Writing down your plan makes it more effective.

The other best ways of coping with the situation includes keeping a drinking diary. Write down in the diary all the time you have a drink, days, weeks, months as well as the number of drinks and the friends that were in the drinking process. Ensure that this diary shows a gradual change in drinking. Ensure that you don't keep any alcohol at home or only keep a very small amount.

It is advisable to eat before drinking. Considering drinking alcohol along with water also makes you drink a smaller amount of alcohol. Other important thing to consider includes taking a break during each drinking activity as well as stopping at some point and relaxing. During the breaks that can be a day or two, take time and rate your emotions as well as how you feel physically. You will find it easier to quit drinking when you have succeeded and your feeling is good!



## Setting Goals and Preparing for Change.

You have now made a decision to commit yourself! I am sure you have seen clearly there is no any advantage associated with drinking and this is why you are here; Congratulations! Once you have successfully made this great decision, you have to move on to goals establishment. This is pertaining to drinking and how you want to stop and quit. You will require to have goals and steps that are clear and realistic-the better way to cope.

You may want to quit drinking all at once, but this can be quite impossible if you have been addicted for a very long time. Your body requires a gradual drinking reduction until you can completely quit. Here consider quitting drinking on some days in the week.  You may decide there will be no drinking at the initial phase for all Sundays then progress and include Saturdays as a no drinking day. You will find that you will progress like that and within three month there will be no any cravings for drinking. If you are a daily drinker you may commit yourself to stop drinking in two days phases.

After you have made the above decision the next step is to decide which day you would wish to start drinking less or stop. This can be the next day, a week after, a month, or even after half a year. Specifying the quitting date is always a very important idea. When you do this in writing it even makes it better. This will add value and help you actually fulfill these plans and goals.

The other important things to consider include ways of overcoming the temptation that will come along the way, how to announce your goal to family members as well as friends, how you will avert the influences that will come along from your past life while you were drinking.

Temptations will come along, but removing anything associated with alcohol around your office and home is quite advisable. This will include alcohol bottles, glasses and other barware. Let members of your family, co-workers, as well as friends get the fact that you have decided to quit drinking.

You can make the decision to attend any occasion where alcohol is served as well as be in company of your "former" drinking friends. Creating a distance with those people who don't give you support in your decision can be very good. This will add more effort on your plans. If it means giving up social and friend connections, let it be! Learning from your previous attempts to stop drinking can also be enlightening. You will be able to know what did not work and what worked. This will also give you some good ways of "pitfalls" avoidance.

## Handling Cravings and Triggers

In the first few months after quitting drinking, you will find it challenging to control the cravings associated with alcohol. This should not stress you nor get you back to alcohol! With proper alcohol treatment you will get best ways of coping with such situations. You will be able to adopt the new life and control the alcohol cravings, social pressures, as well as situations that are stressful.

*Ways of avoiding things that trigger drinking;*

You may start this journey by avoiding areas, people, and activities that initiate alcohol craving. Here you will be required to have a lot of social life changes. Avoidance of buddies that drink is recommended. You can also decide to give up such friends! Don't count that you have lost something; this is a long term gain.

Have the practice of saying "No" to alcoholic drinks during social functions. Generally, you will still find roadblocks to your new lifestyle; you might meet in a social function where alcohol is offered or be forced to attend a friend's bash where you will be offered alcohol. Have the practice of saying, "No Thanks," and pick a non-alcoholic drink to hold in your hand.

The following strategies will assist you in alcohol cravings management.

*How to manage alcohol cravings:*

Initiate a discussion with a person that you trust. This can be a member of the family, alcohol-free friend or sponsor. It should be a person of faith.

Get personal distractions like music listening, going for a walk, performing some housecleaning or even tackling quick tasks. This will give room for the urge to pass.

Always keep reminding yourself on some of the factors that made you not want to drink again. Always "remind your mind" that drinking does not make you feel better.

Accepting the urge can make things better. Ride over it, this is known as urge surfing. It is achieved by meditation. This is something that will crest and then break. After breaking, it will dissipate. When you handle it this way, it will actually cease.


*"Urge surfing" steps*

Start by having an inventory of some of the experiences you have during the craving period. This should be done in writing. Consider sitting down, maybe on a chair in a place that is cool. Breathe inwards quite a number of times and wander your attention throughout the body to feel where you feel the craving. When you notice some of the areas that you are experiencing the urge jot them down. Do this during several cravings.

Focus on each and every area one at a time. You may be feeling numb, tingly or cold. Sometimes hot. Focus on your muscles. Are they relaxed or tensed? What is the size of the involved area? Is there any tension in your mouth or lips? After considering all these factors then you can progress to the last step. This will help you ride it out.

Perform a repetition of the process. Ensure that you keep focus on each of them. Jot down some descriptions on how the changes in these areas happen. Generally people experience cravings in the same area. When you meditate on this, the urge vanishes. This is the natural way of handling craving successfully. Believe me it has worked out for many and it will also work for you!

## Alcohol Addiction Recovery

The time has come to tell you about the most powerful technique I know to change any food related behavior. It is a solution that has the capacity to create an immediate change. With this, I once managed to get one of my friend to quit drinking in only 10 minutes, and I'm not exaggerating.

What we feel about something is determined by what we connect to it. For example, most people are afraid of crocodiles, and the reason is that they associate pain and death with them. The same is true for snakes and a lot of other animals.

Consider what happens when you fall in love. In this situation, you somehow develop an endless list of little details that you adore about the person of your affections. This list usually contains some rather elusive things that wouldn't occur to anyone else.

Remember what I said before: What we feel about something is determined by what we connect to it. So when you fall in love, your mind automatically establishes a wide range of connections that associate every detail of the other person with a good feeling. Suddenly, even disgusting things can be cute.

What would happen if a person afraid of crocodiles or snakes would go through the same process, but consciously? What if this person would choose to look at the best available photography of these animals and ask the following question: Is there something beautiful about this animal?

As I mentioned before, if you ask your brain a question, it will come up with answers. The person might realize that snakes can have brilliant colorations and beautiful patterns in their scales. Furthermore, many species seem to smile like dolphins and their slithering motion often shows great elegance. The person might also come to understand that a snake is very limited, and that its only way to defend itself is to bite, but that it doesn't actually want to. Biting is a waste of their venom, which is their savings account. If they use their venom, they have to hunt and eat to produce more of it. What a snake really wants to do is move away from you, find a mate, curl up and have young. It is not an evil ugly monster.

When it comes to ridding yourself of alcohol, you must do the opposite and recondition your mind to connect bad things with it. If nothing else works for you, this technique will; if it is done properly. It utilizes how the human brain fundamentally connects emotions to things, just like what happens in love.

You may be conditioned to like some aspects of how alcohol takes, how it feels in your mouth, what effects it has on your state of mind or some other qualities.

Instead of these positive things, you need to think of alcohol as the fatty, dirty, liver-destroying, life taking, toxic substance it really is.

I want you to put a bottle of alcohol on the table. Imagine a score from -10 to +10 that measures how much you like this bottle and its content. Gradually, try to imagine, as best as you can, in which state this bottle would have to be in order to score only a 5 on the scale. Then move on to make it only a 3 in your mind, then a 1, then a 0, then a -3 and so on until you finally reach -10.

First, you could imagine that the alcohol is warm, so it definitely isn't a +10. Next, you could imagine that it has been open for too long and that dust is starting to settle on it. Then you could imagine some ants crawling around the bottle, perhaps even floating inside. Imagine that it smells disgusting now, and that it more and more resembles raw oil.

As you go for the negative numbers, you could imagine how other insects start crawling around the bottle. A green shimmering fly that just checked out the garbage is landing on the bottle, also falling inside, followed by some worms and spiders or whatever you want to imagine.

Think of a destroyed, smoking, coal-like liver as the kind of thing the alcohol is doing to your body. Equate alcohol with death, ugliness and disgusting smells. As you go for -10, do the worst mental gore to the bottle of alcohol you can come up with. You could imagine picking it up, smelling a dead animal from its insides, and as you turn it around, worms upon worms start bleeding out of it. You can also imagine that the secret ingredients in alcohol are actually some of the most disgusting things you can come up with.

Once you are done with this exercise, see if you still want to empty the bottle. If you do, repeat the exercise. Repeat it again and again, not only on this day, but the next day. If you recondition what you associate with alcohol, if you associate it with absolute disgust, your brain will accept the new pattern and you will be cured automatically. It can literally be this easy.

While you are using this technique, you can also imagine how nice and refreshing it would be to get away from this disgusting, stinky, insect ridden bottle and drink some pure water. If you feel thirsty upon imagining this, get up and drink some water right after the exercise is done, taking a deep breath afterwards and relishing the pureness and cleanliness of it. Just do it.

This way you will not only connect disgusting images and emotions with the alcohol but also establish the cleanliness of water.

Treatment for alcoholism is something that many people do not seek out. The problem is that many alcoholics do not immediately recognize that they have a problem. Many believe that their drinking is under control. They may rationalize having too much to drink one night as something they did because they had a bad day. They may rationalize drinking all day long as part of vacation, or the weekend, or a special occasion, or to relax. Alcoholics will use anything as an excuse to drink.

Many hide their drinking from others and rationalize that with the thought that other people are judgmental over things that they don't understand. Oftentimes it takes the intervention of an alcoholics loved ones to help them overcome their dependency on alcohol. For those who are suffering from alcoholism or love someone who is suffering from alcoholism, there are different treatment options available.

## Rehabilitation

Many alcoholics find that rehabilitation centers are helpful at helping them overcome their alcohol dependency. The first step to treating alcoholism in rehab is with detoxification. This is the process of removing the alcoholic from all forms of alcohol until their body is finished with withdrawal symptoms. When a person becomes dependent on something such as alcohol, their body cannot stand not having that substance in it. During the withdrawal process, many alcoholics require medication to help them manage their confusion and their visions. This is all done in the presence of medical professionals who are trained to deal with detoxification and withdrawal.

Alcoholics in rehab will meet with counselors who will help them learn what provokes their drinking. There is always an underlying problem that causes people to turn to alcohol. By identifying it and learning what puts them over the edge, alcoholics are taught to avoid that trigger and to turn to something healthy in the future.

Some counseling is done one on one and other counseling is done in a group setting. Group counseling helps people understand their alcoholism, but it also provides support to alcoholics from the counselor and others who are suffering from alcohol abuse. These group sessions provide people with motivation and determination to continue to overcome their alcoholism.

*Medical Treatment for Alcoholism*

There is a medical drug that is designed to help people stop drinking. It won't make them not want to drink, but this drug, called disulfiram, reacts when mixed with alcohol. It makes the person who drinks feel sick. It causes nausea, vomiting, and headaches. Acamprosate is a drug that helps people fight the urge to drink, and naltrexone is a drug that blocks people from feeling happy and light after they drink. In effect, drinking has no effect on those people, which causes them to see no point in drinking.

There are many different treatment options for those who suffer from alcohol abuse. Each one is different and not everyone responds to the same type of treatment, which is why it is important for people to give different treatments a chance before deciding what works.

# Chapter 5: Other Measures to Stop Overdrinking

## Getting Help and Support

Help and support is very essential. It doesn't matter whether you will make the choice of getting it from therapist, outpatient programs, rehab, self-treatment approach or hospitals. All you are required here is never to try to go through it alone. Getting people who you can rely on in terms of guidance, comfort or encouragement can be a great achievement. Consider the fact that you were addicted to alcohol and you are trying to cope with the new situation

None of us are perfect. In dealing with life, and everything that it has to offer, we commit our own fair share of misgivings such as turning to alcohol as a convenient means of escape. What's important, though, is that we learn from our mistakes and that we resolve to become better as a result of the lessons we've picked up along the way.

Perhaps the greatest challenge for any recovering alcoholic is sustaining the positive changes that have been made ever since they decided to quit the bottle. It's never going to be easy. Similar to other forms of addiction, drinking has a tendency to recur over and over again, particularly when the triggers that cause such behavior are not sufficiently addressed and resolved. It is, in other words, a lifetime battle that you should win at every opportunity.

Not everybody has the will to quit alcohol on their own. Even if you come to the point where you realize you have is an addiction, you might find yourself unable to face it head-on and finally put an end to it.

## Joining support groups

One of the most popular ways to overcome alcohol addiction is by joining support groups such as Alcoholics Anonymous or AA. This group follows the 12-step approach to recovery, which is also now being utilized for support groups catering to people who suffer from other forms of addiction. Meetings at AA usually involve sharing of individual stories about how the problem with alcohol dependence started, the factors that triggered it, how it affected one's life, and the steps being done to overcome it.

Much of the success of AA is rooted in the idea that you are not alone in your struggles against alcohol. There are in fact other people who are in the same boat as you are or maybe even in a far worse situation than yours. The fact that you are able to talk about your issues freely, without fear of being judged and with others willing to lend an ear, provides you the outlet that you need to verbalize your problems and eventually conquer them. Listening to the stories of others and how they have managed to rise above their situation also provides you the much-needed reassurance that it is not entirely impossible to get your life back together and start with a clean slate.

Studies show that when combined with other treatments, joining a support group like AA is a more effective way of beating alcoholism than merely undergoing regular treatment. But then again, this remains very subjective because at the end of the day, everything still boils down to your willingness and drive to overcome your condition.

This help or support can be attainable when you rely on counselors, friends, family as well as co-workers and other healthcare providers.

*The following steps will assist you to cope with the support and help care:*

The initial step is making an alliance with family and friends. This is an asset that is invaluable in the process of recovering. In case you have let your loved ones down before, you can opt to seek help from family therapy or couples counseling. All you need is a shoulder to lean on.

Building a social network that is sober gives you another advantage. Making new connections can achieve this in case you revolved in an alcoholic social life. Having friends that are sober ensures that you have support in your process of recovery. Consider joining a civic group, church group, attending events as well as volunteering in social activities.

Make a consideration of moving to a home that has a sober living. This will ensure that you have got place that is supportive, safe as well as convenient for you to live during your process of recovery. Remember that you were addicted to alcohol and thus you need a cool place to relieve the anxiety associated with this. Here you should find an alcohol-free environment for living.

The last step is ensuring that you are attending regular meetings. This should be made a priority. It can be a group where you meet to discuss alcohol and their negative factors so that you will always be reminded. This will also ensure that the people who you spend most of your time with have the understanding of what you are going through in the process of healing and recovery.

## Getting on Track on a Treatment Program

Take advantage of some of the addiction programs and therapies that there are. This is aside from joining the supportive and help groups. There are varied options available although it is also useful to put consideration on some of the following.

Due to the fact that different people react to different types of treatment programs, finding a program that suits you is highly recommended. Have the best therapy or program that is customized to you.

Treatment addresses more than your alcoholic life. Considering the fact that due to addiction there was an effect on your relationships, health, psychology as well as career gives you the importance of seeking treatment. There will be deep examination of your life to ensure everything is in order. This will impact and develop a lifestyle that is new.

Consider seeking help in case you have psychological problems. You will be prescribed to the proper medications or be initiated on a counseling program that will see you through this nightmare. Generally as mentioned earlier alcohol abuse is associated with people who have suffered depression, bipolar disorder, mental problems, attention deficit disorders as well as anxiety. Thus, proper counseling and medication can help.

Aside from the mentioned effects, treatment helps you to have focus and commitment. This is due to the fact that the recovery and alcohol quitting program is not that easy. In case you have been a long term-heavy drinker, consider seeking treatment.

Don't give up; this is a process and it involves very many stages to arrive at the final destination. In case you slip, consider it as a roadblock and try to improve the commitment by reminding yourself why you started this program.

*Rehabilitation facilities*

There are many alcohol rehabilitation and treatment facilities that offer a full suite of services, starting with an alcohol-free environment managed and controlled by medical professionals. These facilities are designed to cater to alcoholics who want to remain sober and push for sobriety over the long term.

The kind of treatment these centers offer varies. Short-term treatments normally include in-patient hospitalization to address the ill effects of withdrawal syndrome. Some centers also have residential services that can be availed of for a very limited time. Long-term treatments, on the other hand, include the full spectrum of services, starting with hospitalization all the way to counseling and therapy.

In any event, availing of treatments, taking in medications to deter alcohol intake, and joining support groups only serve as the first step that you need to take to fully overcome alcohol abuse. What is more important is the need to sustain the positive changes will have made during this period in order to ensure your sobriety over the long term.

*Pharmaceutical options*

Unlike other forms of illnesses, it is important to note that there is no actual medical cure for alcohol dependence. Thankfully, however, there are a number of treatments and interventions available to minimize or altogether mitigate the risks posed by excessive and unabated alcohol intake.

The Food and Drug Administration or FDA, for example, has approved pharmaceutical medicines designed to curb one's tendencies to grab a bottle. These are particularly useful for recovering alcoholics. One of these is Naltrexone (Revia). This drug is taken to reduce alcohol cravings. Another FDA-approved drug is Antabuse (Disulfiram), which makes you sick if you decide to consume alcohol. Lastly, there is Acamprosate (Campral). It eases the discomfort and heavy feelings experienced by addicts following their decision to abstain from alcohol

# Chapter 6: Dealing With the Effects of Withdrawal Syndrome

Deciding to quit the bottle is one thing, but dealing with its effects is another thing altogether. While the former is largely mental and emotional in scope, the latter is predominantly physical. Just the same, though, it is necessary that you remain committed to your goal of becoming alcohol-free no matter the challenges posed by either of these things, including the possibility of having to deal with withdrawal syndrome.

Withdrawal syndrome covers a vast range of physical symptoms, mostly negative, that are experienced by the body as a consequence of ditching alcohol consumption or other addictive substances. It's the body's response to the sudden lack of alcohol in the system. The entire duration of the withdrawal syndrome covers the length of time that the body needs to detoxify and adjust to your modified lifestyle.

## Body detox

More than 90 percent of people who suffer from alcohol abuse are bound to experience mild withdrawal syndrome once they stop drinking. Although uncomfortable and painful in certain instances, the symptoms they experience are manageable and not life-threatening. Some of these symptoms can be rapid heart rate, involuntary trembles or shakes, anxiety and restlessness, excessive sweating, foul body odor, hallucinations and frequent nightmares, bowel movement problems, nausea, chronic tiredness, and loss of appetite.

A small percentage of alcohol addicts, particularly heavy drinkers, experience an extreme form of withdrawal syndrome that can be fatal when left unchecked. The risk of suffering from delirium tremens, a life-threatening condition characterized by extreme convulsions and autonomic instability, is very real for those whose attempts at quitting alcohol were done in an unsustainable fashion. These patients normally need to undergo detoxification treatment. As explained in the previous chapter, sometimes it is a much better option to exercise gradual decrease of alcohol consumption over a period of time rather than stopping immediately. This eases you out of your dependence on alcohol and withdrawal symptoms either don't occur or do so mildly.


## Cleansing stage

The negative effects of withdrawal syndrome are normally at their peak in the few days to a nfew weeks following your decision to quit drinking. During this period, the body undergoes a cleansing stage as it adjusts to your alcohol-free lifestyle. It is important to be mindful of your diet during this period. Stock up on food items rich in essential nutrients such as Vitamin B complex because these are the same nutrients that alcohol prevented from being absorbed by the system.

Getting over the adverse effects of withdrawal syndrome is a critical component that could spell either the success or failure of your fight against alcoholism. After all, it is during this period when your alcohol cravings are at their strongest, with the body looking for alcohol as a way of curing the discomfort and pain it is going through.

# Chapter 7: Starting the Sober Journey Safely

After setting your plans and goals, you are now safe to start you sober life. Whereas quite a number of people will need the help of medical care and supervision to quit drinking, others manage to do so on their own. The option that suits you will only be dependent on the period, frequency as well as rate of your drinking. In some instances, if you have health problems associated with drinking it is advisable to seek medical and health care. All that we are all craving and yearning for is starting a life that is sober in a way that is safe and productive.

According to the health science, the body of a person becomes alcohol dependent when one drinks a lot of it and in a frequent manner. Thus you will be physically dependent on things that are associated with alcohol.

*Some of the alcohol withdrawal symptoms include;*

- Shaking
- Sweating
- Nausea or vomiting
- Headaches
- Increase in blood pressure or increased heart rate
- Concentration and sleeping problems
- Restlessness and anxiety; as well as
- Diarrhea and stomach cramps.

Commonly these symptoms will last for about five days to one week in case you are not a heavy, frequent drinker. Although for those who have been drinking heavily throughout their lives the conditions can cost them their life as situations are normally not that pleasant.

*The following conditions might be evident;*

- Disorientation and confusion
- Severe vomiting

- Fever
- Convulsions or seizures
- Hallucinations
- Extreme agitation

The signs mentioned above come due to alcohol withdrawal that is severe. This might be due to a problem known as DTs, Delirium Tremens. Rarely will you find people with this problem, but in case you fall victim of it in the process, seeking an instant medical attention will give you an optimum care. Actually it might be associated with alteration in the circulation of blood as well as breathing. Alternatively in case you have been drinking throughout your lifetime, seeking a Detox program gives you ultimate results. This is a program that you can take will in hospital, on outpatient basis or in a facility for alcohol treatment. It's the preferred method for heavy drinkers. You will undergo through a medical prescription that will prevent any symptoms or complications that might be associated with the withdrawal and quitting process.

## Greater positivity

Inspire greater positivity in your life by aiming for an improved overall sense of well-being covering your mental, emotional, and physical states.

If your mind is conditioned to grab a drink as a result of stress from work, then it is high time that you develop healthier and more sustainable stress management strategies. A good way to begin is by resorting to easy relaxation techniques that you can perform at your desk such as deep breathing, crushing a stress ball, looking at anything green, going for a quick walk in the park, listening to relaxing music, or practicing alternative relaxation exercises like yoga and tai chi.

Another common trigger for alcoholism is related to psychological problems. If you are drinking as a result of unresolved emotional issues, seek help to identify its root and determine what you need to do in order to alter your prevailing thought patterns. Be proactive in seeking a more holistic perspective.

As for your physical state, try to live an active lifestyle. Allot part of your schedule for regular exercises. Whenever possible, take part in your favorite sports as a productive recreational activity. Working out and being in tiptop condition have been found to boost confidence and improve self-esteem, giving you the positive disposition you need to seek more fruitful and worthwhile endeavors instead of merely grabbing a drink.

Follow this up by being mindful of your diet. This is not only good for your liver, as mentioned before, but eating well and having a full stomach are also an effective way of reducing alcohol cravings.

Engaging in your passions. A great way to keep your mind off alcohol is by engaging in your passions or interests. Find out what you really want to do and dwell on it. The more immersed you are in doing something that you love, the lesser the chances that you experience a relapse.

## Morning Affirmations

A strategy I personally use to get the best out of me is to do affirmations every morning when I get up. What this means is that you say certain sentences, such as: "I intend to live a healthy life and discover more and more healthy foods to eat and enjoy."

I have a long list of such sayings, and by speaking them out loud, my subconscious mind stays aware of them. Thinking isn't enough. If your brain has to verbalize thoughts, it has to work more and automatically pays more attention to the content of those thoughts.

The openings of your affirmations you should use are "I intend" or "I will easily."

"I will easily stay sober. I will easily come to despise alcohol and like healthy foods."

Perhaps you find this silly, but I know a lot of multi-millionaires that do this routine once every day. There are certain things successful people do to that get them where they are, and it is wise to model their behavior.

Never use words like "hope," "could" and such, as these are needy words and make an "if only" statement. You want to be sure of yourself and show your power. The warrior within you has to speak, not a mouse.

There is a second level to affirmations, which is a list of things you are grateful for. Your brain is like a search engine. Most people ask it what's bad about their life, and it will come up with answers. If you ask it what's great about your life, it will come up with answers, too. So make a list of things you are grateful for and speak them every morning. Make a gratitude journal, it helps!

Personally, I have run, ride my bike, or do yoga when I do this, and get ready for the day. You can also just jump a bit on the spot to feel energized, while you say your affirmations. I'm a health coach, writer, and business owner, so I need the energy, the focus, and the clear mind to be at my best every day. What works for me and other busy, successful people is certainly going to work for you.

Lastly, I want to mention that when you wake up, your body is dehydrated and craves nothing more than water. So drink it. No juice, no alcohol, just water. High quality water at best, not just tap water. At least 16 ounces first thing in the morning. Your body will thank you.

Starting a New Lifestyle

Getting a sober mind and life is just a milestone to your alcohol-free life. You actually need to include professional treatment as well as rehab to initiate a new lifestyle that is productive and long-term. You will be required to have a life where drinking has no place; a lifestyle that is meaningful and productive; as well as proper connection with alcohol-free friends, co-workers and family members.

*The following five steps will guide you through your sober lifestyle:*

The first thing is have a proper care of you. This means having a means of mood swings prevention as well as cravings combating. Ensuring that you have slept properly and eaten foods that are right and healthy gives you an addition value. The other thing that you need to incorporate includes regular exercises; this will assist you in relieving stress, releasing endorphins as well as promotion of emotional well-being.

The next step is ensuring that you have built a support network. This will be achieved by surrounding yourself with people of purpose. Ensure that you have social friends, family member as well as co-workers that make you feel good about your new life. This will keep you on the recovery track as well as ensure that you are motivated. All you need is investing in people who help you feel worthy rather than creating embarrassments.

The other key step is new interests and activities development. Here consider finding new hobbies; get to work in areas that have purpose and meaning of sense in your life as well as engaging in volunteer activities. While engaging in such activities there will be no time for drinking in your life. You will find peace as well as fulfillment. This gives you a better feeling.

Consider continuing with the treatment program. In this case ensure that you are engaging in a treatment program, which can be in hospital, outpatient on under drug prescription. You may also have a sponsor or support group that fights against alcoholism.

In case you still have stress, consider dealing with it in ways that are healthy. Don't misguide alcoholism as a way of stress management. You can meditate, exercise, and find techniques for relaxation as well as engaging in breathing exercises to manage your stress. With these steps you will now have started a new lifestyle that is productive.

## Conclusion:

As can be seen above, overdrinking should not be taken lightly. Anyone can fall into alcohol addiction, and it takes a lot of dedication and will power to get out of an addiction. Some people may think alcohol is not very addictive and can always exercise a certain degree of control over it. You can have a few drinks every now and then and your life won't change. This is true, but for many people one or two drinks can be a gateway to alcohol dependence.

Also, we have now learned that one of the greatest dangers of alcohol addiction is not knowing when you've been drinking too much or not realizing when you have a drinking problem.

Therefore, you can use the information in this book to help yourself, friends or loved ones. If you suspect you may be living with or know someone with an alcohol addiction or dependence, you can use the knowledge acquired here to learn the initial signs.  This will give you a base to help them. Making them know or realize they have an alcohol problem is a big step on your part. Or if you discover it for yourself reading this book, then you can make a huge difference in your life.

# About the Author

I'm Dr. Marybeth Crane. I hope you enjoyed this component of my holistic wellness series of short reads. Wellness encompasses not only your physical and mental health, but also your spiritual health and financial health. My main goal in sharing with you my wellness series is to help you attain a happy, healthy life and make age just a number!

I'm a board-certified Podiatric foot and ankle surgeon who has been in private practice, specializing in sports medicine, for over 25 years. I have built a multi-million-dollar private practice and lecture often on business and practice management topics.

I have written several books on running injuries and author a blog at www.myrundoc.com that is solely focused on sports medicine and running topics. I also author a blog on women's health and wellness issues as well as relationships, communication and the issues surrounding the lovely aging process at www.fitfiftyandfabulous.com.

My goal as a motivational speaker is to convince everyone that positive thinking is potent, exercise is the most powerful drug we as physicians can prescribe and choosing a healthy lifestyle will help combat the lovely aging process. I can help you with the small and big changes that will assist you in changing your life for the better! The one percent changes daily are mighty!

In my spare time, I have been competitively running for more than 40 years. It definitely helps burn off the crazy! I have completed more than 20 marathons, a dozen or so Half-Ironman and 2 Full Ironman Triathlons. I have three wonderful daughters and two stepdaughters; so, we also have a boy dog! My husband is truly a saint.

Contact me at marybeth@fitfiftyandfabulous.com. Follow me @myrundoc on Twitter, @fitfiftyandfabulous on Facebook, and @myrundoc.crane on Instagram. I look forward to your questions and comments.

If Your Running Feet Could Talk
Change Your Attitude, Change Your Life: The Power of Optimism
Stress Relief Meditation
The Money Cleanse
Stop Procrastinating: How to Get Your Sh*t Done!
Stop Overdrinking: Rethinking Your Relationship with Alcohol
Self-Motivation: How to Get Motivated, Stay Motivated and Live Motivated
Coming Soon: Finding Your Purpose

www.ingramcontent.com/pod-product-compliance
Lightning Source LLC
Chambersburg PA
CBHW051122250726
48655CB00007B/2842